•Fun with English•
English Usage

George Beal
Illustrated by Peter Stevenson

GORILLA GUERRILLA

Chambers

D1076898

General editor: John Grisewood
Illustrations: Peter Stevenson
   (Kathy Jakeman Illustration)
Design: Robert Wheeler Associates

CHAMBERS
An imprint of Larousse plc
Elsley House, 24–30 Great Titchfield Street,
London W1P 7AD

This edition published by Chambers 1995
2 4 6 8 10 9 7 5 3 1

The material in this edition was previously published
by Kingfisher Books in the *Wordmaster* series (1993)
and in the *Kingfisher Book of Words* (1991)

This edition copyright © Larousse plc 1995
Copyright © Grisewood & Dempsey Ltd 1991, 1993

All rights reserved. No part of this publication may
be reproduced, stored in a retrieval system or
transmitted by any means, electronic, mechanical,
photocopying or otherwise, without the prior
permission of the publisher.

A CIP catalogue record for this book is available
from the British Library

ISBN 0 550 325042

Printed in Spain

CLASS NO J428 BEA
ITEM NO 3300313386
THE LIBRARY
WESTMINSTER COLLEGE
OXFORD OX2 9AT

Although English grammar is not as difficult as the grammar of many other European languages, English does present some difficulties, and even good speakers and writers are sometimes inclined to make mistakes. For example, you hear on radio or television someone telling you that 'we need less people to work in factories or offices'. This is wrong. What should have been said was 'we need *fewer* people'. The word 'people' refers not to a substance, such as sugar, but to separate things. This listing will warn you of a few of the pitfalls in English, and help you to overcome them.

a, an The indefinite article. *A* is used before a noun which starts with a consonant, as in *a book, a ship, a building*; while *an* is used before a noun which starts with a vowel, as in *an earwig, an egg, an article*. Before words beginning with a silent *h*, the word *an* is used, as in *an honour, an hour, an heir*.

abbreviations Shortened forms of words and phrases (*see box*).

-able, -ible These suffixes can be added to certain verbs and nouns to form adjectives. Examples of the *-able* suffix are: *bearable, readable, reliable, passable*. If the suffix *-able* is added to words ending in *e*, the *e* is usually dropped, but there are some words which can be spelled both ways, for example: *blamable* or *blameable, likable* or *likeable, livable* or *liveable, sizable* or *sizeable, unshakable* or *unshakeable*. Examples of words with the *-ible* suffix are: *accessible, audible, collapsible, compatible, credible, digestible, divisible, edible, eligible, fallible, flexible, indelible, intelligible, possible, visible*.

above and **over** The first word means 'at a higher level than', and the second word means 'on top of'. Sometimes both can mean the same thing, for example: 'Mr and Mrs Singh lived *over* [*or above*] the shop'.

abbreviations	
a.m.	before noon (*ante meridiem*)
BA	Bachelor of Arts
BSc	Bachelor of Sciences
cm	centimetre(s)
Dr	doctor
etc.	and so on (*et cetera*)
GB	Great Britain
kg	kilogramme(s)
kph	kilometres per hour
l	litre(s)
m	metre(s)
mph	miles per hour
Mr	Mister
Mrs	Mistress
NB	take note (*nota bene*)
p	page
p.m.	after noon (*post meridiem*)
pp	pages
rpm	revolutions per minute
RSVP	please reply (*répondez s'il vous plaît*)
sae	stamped addressed envelope
UK	United Kingdom
USA	United States of America
v	against (*versus*)

abstract and concrete Abstract nouns are names of things which cannot be touched, but only thought about. Concrete nouns are actual things which exist. Examples of abstract nouns are: *fear, anger, speed, freedom, happiness, patience, honesty*. The following are examples of concrete nouns: *box, railway, school, girl, country*; in fact anything which you can see, touch or hear.

accent This refers to the syllable which is stressed in a word. In the following examples the stress or accent is shown by printing the accented syllable in capital letters: *TAIlor, INsect, STORy, reQUEST, HAPpiness, aLARM, imMEDiate*. Sometimes, when a word can be used as both a noun and verb, the accent or stress changes. You set an example by good *CONduct*, but you *conDUCT* an orchestra.

accept and **except** *Accept* is a verb, and means 'to take or receive', while *except* is a preposition meaning 'other than' or 'apart from'.

TAIL-OR

acetic and **ascetic** The first word refers to *acetic* acid, which is similar to vinegar. The second word means someone who practises self-denial.

acronym A word made up of the initials, or part-syllables of a phrase (*see box*).

AD and **BC** AD stands for *Anno Domini*, Latin for 'in the year of the Lord' and BC stands for 'before Christ'. AD should be written before the year, as in 'AD 1984', while BC should be written after the year, as in '96 BC'

adjective An adjective describes things, ideas or living beings and is often used to give more information about a noun. Here are some examples of adjectives: 'That is a *fast* car', 'What a *pretty* flower!', 'I eat from a *wooden* table'. Adjectives can be formed from nouns and verbs (*see box*). Adjectives formed from proper nouns take a capital letter: *American, Swedish, Christian, Jewish*.

---

acronyms
AIDS: **a**cquired **i**mmune **d**eficiency **s**yndrome
laser: **l**ight **a**mplifications by **s**timulated **e**mission of **r**adiation
Nato: **N**orth **A**tlantic **T**reaty **O**rganization
Oxfam: **Ox**ford Committee for **Fam**ine Relief
radar: **ra**dio **d**etection **a**nd **r**anging
sonar: **so**und **na**vigation **r**anging
Unesco: **U**nited **N**ations **E**ducational, **S**cientific and **C**ultural **O**rganization

Adjectives
formed from nouns:

acrobat	acrobatic
arch	arched
bride	bridal
character	characteristic
color	colorful
emotion	emotional
friend	friendly
gold	golden
juice	juicy
monster	monstrous
navy	naval
picture	picturesque
reflex	reflexive
water	watery

formed from verbs:

collapse	collapsible
defend	defensive
eat	eatable
love	lovable
possess	possessive

adverse and **averse** The first word means 'unfavourable', while the second means 'unwilling, against or opposed to'. Examples are: 'He had an *adverse* report from his school', 'What boy or girl is *averse* to eating ice-cream?'.

affect and **effect** The first word is a verb, and means 'to act upon or influence', while the second word can be either a noun and mean 'the result or consequence of an action', or a verb meaning 'to bring about'. Here are some examples: 'Your advice will *affect* my decision', 'We sent Lucy to a new school, which had a good *effect* on her behaviour', 'The prisoner had *effected* his escape'.

adverbs
early
finally
never
slowly
sometimes
wearily
yesterday

admit This verb can mean two quite different things. The first meaning is 'to confess or acknowledge' a sin or crime, and the second is 'to allow to enter'.

adverb An adverb describes a verb and tells how, when or where something happens, for example: *carefully, easily, visibly, truthfully, happily.* You can say that 'Jim writes *beautifully*' or 'Hannah sings *superbly*'. These adverbs are easy to recognize because they end in 'ly'. But not all adverbs do. Here are some more examples of adverbs which tell how, when or where: 'He *always* gets cross if you argue with him', 'Ann wants you to telephone her *now*', 'I like eating *here*'.

A PRISONER EFFECTING HIS ESCAPE

5

afflict and **inflict** The first word means 'to trouble or pain', while the second means 'to impose or enforce, or to cause suffering'. Examples are: 'My mother is badly *afflicted* by rheumatism', 'The enemy planes bombed the town, *inflicting* much loss of life'.

aggravate This word is often used to mean 'to annoy or irritate', such as in the sentence 'My little brother often *aggravates* me'. However, its proper meaning is 'to make worse', as in the sentence: 'Her bad cold was *aggravated* by the damp climate'.

alphabetical order It is sometimes useful to list items or names in *alphabetical order*. To do this, you should take each letter as it appears, ignoring spaces, hyphens and other marks, such as apostrophes.

Look first at the initial letters of the words you wish to alphabetize and arrange them in the order of the alphabet, for example: *lion* would come before *mother, water* after *vole*. If several words start with the same letter, or group of letters, look in turn at the second, third, fourth etc. letters of the word. For example, *move, mouse, moat, moan* and *more* arranged into alphabetical order give the following list *moan, moat, more, mouse, move*.

Names beginning with *Mac, Mc* or *M'* should all be regarded as if they were spelled *Mac*. The abbreviation *St* for 'Saint' should be treated as if it were spelled out: *Saint Matthew*. Similarly, names like *S. Pedro* and *S. Maria* should be treated as if the names were spelled in full: *San Pedro* and *Santa Maria*. Abbreviations such as EC, NATO or UNESCO should be treated as if they are ordinary words, and placed alphabetically as they appear.

already and **all ready** These two should not be confused. *Already* is an adverb, as used in the sentence 'The shops were *already* open by the time I reached the centre'. *All ready* is an adjectival phrase, as used in the sentence 'We were *all ready* to depart when John arrived'.

altar and **alter** The first word means a table or structure in a church, while the second means 'to change something'.

anagram An *anagram* is a word formed by using the letters of one word rearranged to form one or more other words. Here are some examples: *angle* can be rearranged to make the word *glean, pirates* can be rearranged to spell *sea trip*, and *telegraph* can be rearranged to make *great help*.

anagrams

nameless	salesmen
despair	praised
it ran	train
infection	fine tonic
punishment	nine thumps
solemn	melons
night	thing

& [and] This symbol is called an *ampersand*, and means simply *and*. However, its use should be limited to the names of firms or companies: *Henry Robinson & Co., Babcock & Wilcox.*

ante and **anti** These two prefixes mean quite different things. The first means 'before' and the second means 'against or opposed to'. An *anteroom* is a small room giving access to a larger one. *Anti-clockwise* means 'in the opposite direction to the rotation of the hands of a clock'.

antonym An antonym is a word which gives the opposite meaning to another (*see box*).

antonyms

advance	retreat
clean	dirty
clever	stupid
covered	uncovered
deep	shallow
freedom	captivity
giant	dwarf
help	hinder
hope	despair
light	dark
low	high
obey	disobey
slow	quick
swim	sink
thick	thin
under	over
up	down

apostrophe ['] This is a punctuation mark, and is used to show contractions when letters are omitted, for example, *don't* for 'do not'. It is also used to indicate the possessive form of nouns and some pronouns, for example: *Joseph's brother, the girls' shoes, a week's holiday.*

artist and **artiste** The first word refers to someone like a painter, sculptor or musician, while the second refers to someone who works as an entertainer, such as a singer or comedian.

as *As* should not usually be used as an alternative word to *because*. For instance 'I cannot come to your party as I am going to the doctor' could mean that the writer could not come to the party *on his way* to the doctor! In this case the word *as* should be replaced by *because*.

7

B

balmy and **barmy** The first of these words means 'sweet-smelling' or 'mild and pleasant'. The second is a slang word, meaning 'silly or foolish'. Although both words are sometimes spelled 'balmy', it is better to use the second spelling for the meaning 'foolish'.

because This word means 'for the reason that'. *Because* is sometimes replaced by *as* or *since*, especially at the beginning of sentences: '*As* you've come such a long way, perhaps you'd like to stay to dinner?', '*Since* you ask, I must tell you that I shall be leaving tomorrow'.

beside and **besides** *Beside* means 'by the side of', and *besides* means 'in addition' or 'moreover': 'I do like to be *beside* the seaside', 'I didn't like that house, and *besides*, it was on the wrong side of the road'.

biannual and **biennial** *Biannual* means 'twice a year', and *biennial* means 'occurring every two years'.

bizarre and **bazaar** The first word means 'odd or unusual' from the Italian *bizzarro*. The second means 'a type of market' from the Persian word for a market *bazar*.

buffet There are two words spelled in this way. The first refers to a bar or counter where food is served. In this case, the word is a French one and is pronounced *bu-fay*, while the second is pronounced *buffit* and means 'to strike or knock something'.

C

calendar, **calender** and **colander** A *calendar* is something which tells you the date, a *calender* is a machine which smooths cloth or paper, and a *colander* is a kitchen utensil used for draining vegetables.

can and **may** The word *can* means 'ability to do something', while *may* means 'to have permission to'. For example: '*Can* I leave school early today?' means 'am I able to leave school early today?'. The answer to that is, 'yes, you are *able* to do so, but you still need permission!'. The correct question is: '*May* I leave school early today?'.

PLEASE MISS, MAY I LEAVE SCHOOL EARLY TODAY?

8

cancel and **postpone** *Cancel* means 'to call off completely', while *postpone* means 'to put off until another time'.

capital letters Capital letters are used in the following cases:

For proper nouns and their adjectives: *Henry Jones, Mrs Edith Johnson, Uncle Harry, Germany, German, Bovril, the United States, American, Marxist.*

At the beginning of a sentence: *All sentences begin with a capital letter.*

For the names of the days of the week, months of the year and festivals: *January, Monday, Christmas Day.*

For titles of people: *Her Majesty, Lord Williams, President Bush.*

For the name of God: *God, Allah.*

For the titles of books, newspapers, plays, films etc: *Charlie and the Chocolate Factory, The Great Gatsby, The Mousetrap, The Times.*

cereal and **serial** A *cereal* is a plant from which grain, such as oats, barley or wheat, is produced, while a *serial* is a story told in episodes or parts.

chord and **cord** A *chord* is a musical term which refers to sounding several notes together, while *cord* is a kind of rope or string.

clause A *clause* is a sentence which is part of a larger sentence. For instance, 'Jane spoke to Henry and Bill took Mary's arm' is one sentence, but it contains two shorter sentences or *clauses: Jane spoke to Henry* and *Bill took Mary's arm*. These two *clauses* are joined together by the word 'and' to make one sentence. *Clauses* can be linked by other words, too. In 'I was in the shop when I saw Joe', the first *clause: I was in the shop* is linked to the second *I saw Joe* by the word *when*.

clichés A *cliché* is a phrase or sentence which is so often used that it has become boring and commonplace. It is best to avoid *clichés* if you can, particularly in written work. Here are some which are often heard: *as good as gold, a blessing in disguise, explore every avenue, leave no stone unturned, the wind of change.*

coarse and **course** *Coarse* means 'rough or unrefined', while *course* means 'a track where races are held' or 'a series of lessons'.

colon [:] This is a punctuation mark. It is used to separate clauses in a sentence, when the second part explains or reveals the first. For example: 'Alison was very unhappy: she had lost her kitten', 'Tom could not get into his house: he had the wrong key'. You can also use colons to precede a list, 'I suggest you buy some vegetables: onions, potatoes and cabbage'.

comma [,] This is a punctuation mark. It is used in the following ways:

To separate a series of things or items: 'We are going to Europe and will visit France, Germany, Italy and Spain', 'Would you like tea, coffee, milk or cocoa?'.

Between a number of adjectives before a noun: 'What a nice, pleasant, intelligent person!', 'The film was fantastic, exciting, entertaining and full of adventure'.

To separate clauses in a sentence: 'My friend Raji, who has dark hair, has just won a school prize', 'Jack, would you please come to my room?'.

In a list it is usual to omit the comma at the end after the last word before *and* and *or*, and before the final noun.

comparatives A *comparative* is a form of an adjective or adverb which indicates 'more'. It is formed by adding *-er, -est, more* or *most*. The first form of an adjective is called the *positive*, the second is called the *comparative* and the third is called the *superlative*. Here are examples of the three, using the adjective 'quick':

'This is the quick way into town.'
[positive]
'This is the quicker way into town.'
[comparative]
'This is the quickest way into town.'
[superlative]

You should use the *comparative* when **two** items are being discussed. In the example above, if there were only two ways into town, you would have said that one was *quicker* than the other. If there were three or more, you would have used the *superlative*.

Another example is: 'We have two guinea-pigs at home and the brown one is *the largest*'. This is wrong, since you cannot have the *largest* of two. The correct sentence should read: 'We have two guinea-pigs at home and the brown one is *the larger*'. The following sentence is correct: 'I am *the tallest* boy in my school' because it can be assumed that there are more than two boys in the school.

Sometimes, it is not possible to add *-er* or *-est* to the adjective or adverb. Take the word *beautiful*. You cannot say *beautifuler*. Instead, you should say *more beautiful*, as in: 'My sister is *more beautiful* than her cousin'. Or, for the superlative, 'My sister is the *most beautiful* girl in the family'.

competition and **contest** The word *contest* is mostly used for something which is officially organized, while *competition* is considered rather more informal. For example: 'Fred hopes to win the "best singer" *contest* next month. I expect there will be a lot of *competition* to get seats'.

complement and **compliment** The first word means 'a complete amount', while the second means 'a remark expressing admiration'. For example: 'We went to

WE HAVE TWO GUINEA-PIGS AT HOME, AND THE GREY ONE IS THE LARGEST

sea with a full *complement* of crew', 'Jenny was pleased at the *compliment* when her teacher said that her drawing was the best she had seen'.

conjunction A *conjunction* is a word which links two or more other words, clauses or sentences (*see box*). A *conjunction* can be used to join words, such as in 'bread *and* butter', 'slow *but* sure', 'ugly *yet* attractive'. Another use is to connect phrases: 'He wants to learn *but* is too lazy to try', 'Jodie likes Jon *because* he is so kind'.

continual and **continuous** The first word means 'recurring frequently, especially at regular intervals', while the second means 'unceasing, without break'. For example: '*Continuous* work is impossible if there are *continual* interruptions'.

conjunctions	
after	if
although	or
and	since
because	until
before	when
but	yet

contraction This is a shortening of words by combining them together with an apostrophe [']. The apostrophe shows where a letter or letters are missing. Here are some examples: I am – *I'm*; she is – *she's*; you are – *you're*; cannot – *can't*; is not – *isn't*; shall not – *shan't*.

It is important to place the apostrophe in the right position. It should indicate where the letter or letters are missing.

council and **counsel** The word *council* refers to 'an assembly of people', while *counsel* means 'advice or guidance'. For example: 'The city *council* meets once a month', 'I always take *counsel* from a friend if I need help'.

curb and **kerb** The first word means 'to check or hold back', while the second refers to the edging stone of a pavement. In the United States, both words are usually spelled *curb*.

currant and **current** The first word means 'a type of dried fruit', and the second 'most recent, up-to-date' or 'a flow of water or electricity'.

decimate This word is often used to mean 'to do great damage or to kill many people'. In fact, the original meaning was 'to destroy one person in ten'.

dependant and **dependent** The word *dependant* is a noun which means 'someone who depends on another person for aid', while *dependent* is an adjective and means 'depending on'. For example: 'Their *dependants* were *dependent* upon them for food and clothing'. In the United States, both words are often spelled *dependent*.

desert and **dessert** The first word means 'an arid, uncultivated place', while *dessert* is a pudding, usually the last course in a meal.

desiccate This word is frequently misspelled. It has one *s* and two *c*'s.

11

different to, **from**, **than** *Different from* is the most usual and acceptable form of this expression, although *different to* and, in the United States, *different than* are sometimes used.

dinghy and **dingy** These two words are pronounced differently and mean different things. *Dinghy* (pronounced with a hard 'g' as in 'get') is a small boat, while *dingy* (pronounced with a soft 'g' as in 'gin') means 'drab or shabby'.

diphthong This word describes two vowels which are joined together and pronounced as one. Examples are *au, ou, ea, oi, ow, aw*. The letter *w* in these cases counts as a vowel.

discomfit and **discomfort** The word *discomfit* means 'to make uneasy or confused; to frustrate or defeat'. *Discomfort* is usually a noun and means 'inconvenience, distress or mild pain'. It can sometimes be used as a verb, when it means 'to make uncomfortable or cause distress'.

discreet and **discrete** *Discreet* means 'careful to avoid embarrassment', while *discrete* means 'separate or distinct'.

disinterested and **uninterested** These two words do not mean the same thing. *Disinterested* means 'free from bias; impartial', while *uninterested* means 'indifferent or having no interest in something; bored'.

double negative Negatives are such words as *no, not, neither, never, nothing, nobody, nowhere*. Examples of *double negatives* in sentences are: 'I *didn't* do *nothing* wrong', 'I *haven't never* been lost'. They are wrong because the two negatives cancel each other out. Correctly, the two sentences should read, 'I *did nothing* wrong', or 'I *didn't* do *anything* wrong' and 'I *have never* been lost'.

There are some instances where *double negatives* can be used correctly. 'It is *not unusual* to see a rainbow' or 'I am *not ungrateful* for your help' are both perfectly good English.

drink The past tense of *drink* is *drank*. The past participle is *drunk*. As an adjective, the word is *drunken* and sometimes *drunk*. For example: 'He *drank* some wine', 'He has *drunk* some wine', 'The soldiers were *drunk*', 'A group of *drunken* soldiers entered the town'. It would be incorrect to say 'He *drunk* the wine'.

BUT I DIDN'T DO NOTHING WRONG

SWAG

eatable and **edible** *Eatable* implies that something is not only fit to eat, but enticing, while *edible* means simply 'fit to eat without harm'.

e.g. and **i.e.** The first is an abbreviation of the Latin *exempli gratia*, which means 'for example'; while the second, again Latin, comes from *idem est*, meaning 'that is to say'. The two expressions are not interchangeable. For example: 'We have a great selection of garden flowers, *e.g.* fuchsias, roses, geraniums and lilies'. Whereas 'I expect the exhibition will attract large numbers of philatelists, *i.e.* stamp collectors'.

-ei- There is an old spelling rule which says '*i* before *e* except after *c*'. It is true in the majority of cases (*see box*), but there are a number of other words which use *ei*: *counterfeit, deign, either, feign, foreign, freight, height, kaleidoscope, leisure, neighbour, neither, reign, seize, sleigh, their* and *vein* are just a few. There are also some words in which *ie* follows *c*, for example: *ancient, glacier, science* and *species*.

-ei- words	
ceiling	deceive
conceivable	perceive
conceive	receipt
deceipt	receive

either This word is applied to one of two persons or things. For example: 'You can have *either* tea or coffee'. *Either* is a singular word, as shown in the following sentence: '*Either* Charles or Harry *was* to be considered', not '*Either* Charles or Harry *were* to be considered'. The same rule also applies to *neither* and *nor*.

elder and **older** The word *elder* is used when you are speaking of people from the same family, such as in 'Celia is the *elder* of our two daughters'. In other circumstances, you should use *older*, as in 'My friend Celia is *older* than she looks', 'That theatre is *older* than any other building in the town'. The same rules apply to *eldest* and *oldest*.

eligible and **illegible** The word *eligible* means 'worthy or qualified'; *illegible* means 'difficult to read'.

enormity and **immensity** The word *enormity* means 'an atrocity, an act of great wickedness', as in the sentence 'The judge considered the *enormity* of the prisoner's crimes and sentenced him to a long period of imprisonment'. *Enormity* is often used incorrectly to mean 'greatness' or 'a great amount'. The correct word in this case is *immensity*, for example, 'She hadn't realized the *immensity* of the problem'.

rules are there to be broken!

ensure and **insure** The first word means 'to make certain or sure', while the second means 'to guarantee or protect against risk'. In the United States both words are spelled *insure*.

eponym This is a word which is taken from someone's name (*see box*).

-ess This is a suffix which is often added to words to denote a feminine person or animal. Many of these words are rarely used, for example *authoress, conductress, editress, manageress, poetess, sculptress*. Women are now given the same titles as men: *author, conductor, editor, manager, poet,*

> **eponyms**
> boycott: Captain Boycott
> braille: Louis Braille
> leotard: Jules Léotard
> magnolia: Pierre Magnol
> maverick: Samuel Augustus Maverick
> plimsoll: Samuel Plimsoll
> teddy bear: Theodore (Teddy) Roosevelt
> sandwich: Earl of Sandwich
> shrapnel: General Shrapnel
> wellingtons: Duke of Wellington

sculptor. A few *-ess* words, such as *actress, hostess, stewardess, waitress*, remain, and the feminine form of titles such as *baroness, countess, duchess, empress, goddess, princess* are still used. Some words ending in *-ess* are male, *marquess*, for instance.

euphemisms A *euphemism* is an attempt to make something unpleasant sound less so by substituting different words. For instance, instead of saying 'she has died', you might say 'she has passed away'. Many people try to avoid saying certain words, for example using *tummy* instead of 'belly', the *smallest room* for 'toilet' or 'loo', *perspire* for 'sweat' and *stout* instead of 'fat'.

exclamation mark [!] This is a punctuation mark. It is used at the end of a sentence to express surprise, amusement, disagreement or a command. For example: 'Hooray!', 'Get out!', 'What fun!', 'Don't you dare to speak to me like that!'. It is never advisable to use too many *exclamation marks* in written work, since they will lose their impact. Never confuse an *exclamation mark* with a question mark. 'Whoever did that?' is a question, not an exclamation.

THE DUKE OF WELLINGTON

faint and **feint** *Faint* has two meanings. As an adjective it means 'unclear or not bright'. As a verb it means 'to lose consciousness'. *Feint*, on the other hand, means 'a mock attack or movement'.

fantastic Although it is often used in this sense, strictly *fantastic* does not mean 'wonderful' or 'excellent'. To say 'we had a *fantastic* time in America' is incorrect if what is meant is 'we had a *great* time in America'. The word *fantastic* actually means 'strange or fanciful'.

farther and **further** If you are talking about distance, then *farther* should be used, as in 'Moscow is *farther* from London than from Berlin'. In other senses only *further* can be used, for example: 'are there any *further* questions?' or '*further* to my remarks yesterday, I have one suggestion to make'.

fatal and **fateful** *Fatal* means 'resulting in death', while *fateful* means 'having momentous consequences or controlled by fate'.

fewer and **less** *Fewer* means 'smaller in number', and *less* means 'a smaller quantity or amount'. These two words are often confused. You might hear someone say: 'We shall need *less* people to do this job' but this is incorrect because people are counted in numbers, not in quantity. The correct sentence should be: 'We shall need *fewer* people to do this job'. If you are dealing with an amount, then you should say, for instance: 'This recipe needs *less* sugar'. Again, you would be wrong in saying: 'I shall buy *less* apples this week', because apples are a number of separate things. The sentence should be: 'I shall buy *fewer* apples this week'.

figurative language can take many forms. *Figures of speech* are ways of expressing something by other means than the literal truth. You can use *irony*, which is a way of saying something when you actually mean the opposite, such as in 'you're a fine one to talk!' You can employ *paradox*, which is saying something which is apparently nonsense, but which really makes sense, such as 'make haste slowly', or 'the child is father of the man'. You can use *metaphors*, such as 'the kettle is boiling' and 'a bed of roses'. In each of these cases, you understand a meaning. You know that it is the water which is boiling, not the kettle, and that the bed of roses has nothing to do with roses at all, but describes something pleasant.

full stop/full point [.] The full stop or full point is a punctuation mark and is placed at the end of a sentence. It is also used to denote that a word is abbreviated, as in *no.* for 'number', or *Dr.* for 'doctor'. The full stop or full point is also known as the 'period', or sometimes just as a 'point'. It is now quite common for the full stop to be omitted after some abbreviations such as *Mr, Mrs, mph, anon.*

fulsome does not mean 'very full'. It means 'nauseous, excessive or insincere'. It comes from the Old English *fulsom* meaning 'copious' and 'cloying'.

15

GORILLA GUERRILLA

gender Many languages, such as French, German and Latin, have masculine and feminine nouns. In French, for example, the word for 'table' is feminine, *la table*, but 'fire' is masculine, *le feu*.

Gender does not apply in English, but there are some nouns which refer specifically to a masculine or feminine person or animal, for example: *bride,* *groom; goose, gander; ram, ewe; cock, hen*. There are also some nouns which change their form depending upon the gender of the subject they are naming: *actor, actress; waiter, waitress; god, goddess; prince, princess.*

Gender is also used in English pronouns: *he, him his* are the masculine forms; *she, her hers* are the feminine forms. The neuter forms, describing a thing rather than a person or animal, are *it* and *its.*

glasnost This is a Russian word which has only recently entered the English language. It means 'openness'.

gorilla and **guerilla** *Gorilla* is the name of a particular species of great apes, while *guerilla* (sometimes spelled *guerrilla*) is 'a member of an irregular army'.

gourmand and **gourmet** These two words have similar meanings, but there is one big difference. *Gourmand* is an unflattering term and means 'a glutton, or someone who likes food but eats greedily', while *gourmet* means 'someone who likes food but who is discriminating and careful as to how or what they eat'.

grill and **grille** A *grill* is a plate or bars placed above heat for cooking meat or other food. The word can also be used as a verb, *to grill*, which describes the way such food is cooked. A *grille* is a framework of metal bars over a window.

grisly, **gristly** and **grizzly** The first word, *grisly*, means 'horrible or gruesome'. *Gristly* means 'containing much gristle'. *Grizzly* means 'grey' and is applied to a particular sort of bear, the *grizzly bear*, because of its colour.

hail and **hale** The word *hail* as a noun means 'frozen rain pellets'; as a verb it means 'to greet' or 'to be native to a particular country'. The word *hale* means 'healthy or robust'.

hangar and **hanger** A *hangar* is 'a building for storing aircraft', and a *hanger* is 'a support for something hanging', such as a *coat hanger*.

hiccup and **hiccough** The first word is the correct spelling, although the second is commonly used.

hoard and **horde** The first word means 'an accumulated store', and the second means 'a vast crowd'.

homonym *Homonym* comes from two Greek words meaning 'the same' and 'name'. A homonym is therefore a word which has the same sound as another, but which has a different meaning, and usually a different spelling. For instance: *right, rite, write* and *wright* all sound the same, but have quite different meanings. A word which sounds the same as another but is spelled differently is known as a *homophone* (*see box*). A word which has several different meanings is called a *homograph* for example: 'She was in the *right*', 'I told him to turn *right* at the end of the road'.

hyperbole This word, which is taken from the Greek, is pronounced 'hyPERbolee' and means 'a figure of speech which uses exaggeration to make its point'. Here are some examples of *hyperbole*: 'A thousand

homophones	
beer	bier
here	hear
lie	lye
meet	meat
scull	skull
sum	some
sun	son
there	their
wait	weight
ware	wear

apologies', 'You'll die laughing when you hear this!', 'She cried her eyes out'.

hyphen Hyphens are mostly used to indicate that two or more words should be regarded as one, such as *fall-out, ice-cream, frying-pan, happy-go-lucky, good-for-nothing, stick-in-the-mud*. A hyphen is also used with certain prefixes, such as *co-* or *re-*, in words like *co-operate*, and *re-count* which means 'to count again', to avoid confusion with the word *recount* which means 'to tell a story'. A hyphen is also used in books to show where a word-break appears at the end of a line.

illegible and **unreadable** The word *illegible* is an adjective and means 'difficult to read, because it is faint or badly printed'. *Unreadable*, also an adjective, means 'badly-worded or very dull'.

inapt and **inept** The word *inapt* means 'unsuitable', while the word *inept* means 'awkward or clumsy'.

17

incredible and **incredulous** The first word, *incredible*, means 'beyond belief or understanding', while *incredulous* means 'unwilling to believe something'.

infinitive This is the word used to describe the basic 'name' of a verb. In English, this usually takes a form starting with *to*. The following are some *infinitives* of verbs: *to walk, to ride, to eat, to sleep, to be, to go*. The word *to* is omitted when the verb follows some other, auxiliary (or helping) verbs: *I must go, we might win, you may speak, they have gone*.

If an adverb or phrase comes between the word *to* and the verb, such as in *to rarely be, to quickly eat, to in some way run, to almost always sit*, it is called a *split infinitive*. Some people regard a split infinitive as a grammatical error, but this is not the case. The famous line '*to boldly go* where no man has gone before', which comes from the TV series 'Star Trek', is another typical case of a *split infinitive*.

It is best to word a sentence in the most elegant way, whether the infinitive is split or not. In fact, there are times when it is almost impossible to write a sentence without splitting the infinitive. In the sentence, 'In my new job I hope *to more than double* my salary', the phrase 'more than' cannot be moved elsewhere in the sentence without destroying the meaning.

inflammable and **flammable** Both these words mean the same thing: 'liable to catch fire and burn easily'. It is possible to mistake the meaning of the first word for 'unlikely to burn, or non-burnable', so some people think that it is better always to use the word *flammable* to avoid confusion.

ingenious and **ingenuous** The word *ingenious* means 'skilful or clever', and the word *ingenuous* means 'naïve or innocent'.

interjection This is a term used in grammar to describe a particular type of word. *Interjections* express an exclamation and, in fact, are usually followed by an exclamation mark: '*Hooray!*', '*Alas!*', '*Oh!*'. Some *interjections* contain more than one word, such as: '*Oh, dear!*', '*Good gracious!*'. *Interjections* can be part of a sentence too: 'Fred, *alas*, was late as usual' (*see box*).

interjections	
Hooray!	Good gracious!
Alas!	Great!
Oh!	Phew!
Ah!	Ugh!
Hey!	Well I never!
Oh dear!	

invite This is a verb, and means 'to ask someone politely and graciously'. The noun is *invitation* and is something you can send, or offer, by word of mouth. It is wrong to use *invite* as a noun, as in 'I'll send you an *invite*' and this should always be avoided.

its and **it's** The first word is the possessive form of the word *it*, and is used in such sentences as: 'The elephant lifted *its* trunk above *its* head'. The word *it's* is a contraction or shortening of the two words *it is*, as can be seen in the sentence: '*It's* not easy to pass examinations'. The two words are often confused, but it is wrong to use one in place of the other.

THE ELEPHANT LIFTED ITS TRUNK ABOVE ITS HEAD

L

lama and **llama** A *lama* is a Buddhist monk, and a *llama* is a South American animal of the camel family.

lath and **lathe** A *lath* is a strip of wood, while a *lathe* is a machine for turning wood, metal or similar material.

lay and **lie** These are two different verbs. The problem is that the past tense of *lie* is *lay*, which is why the two verbs are sometimes confused. The verb *to lie* means 'to recline, rest or be horizontal'. The verb *to lay* means 'to put down, or to deposit, or to place'. Here are some examples of the use of the verb *to lie*: 'I am going *to lie down*', 'It is a warm day, I *shall lie* in the sun', 'Yesterday, I *lay* in bed thinking'. The word *lay* here is the past tense. Now, here are some examples of the use of the word *to lay*. 'After you finish reading, *lay* the book down', 'I'm sure I

laid my pencil on this table yesterday'. The word *laid* here is the past tense.

There is, of course, another verb *to lie*, which means 'not to tell the truth'. In the present tense, this takes the form *lie, lies, lying*, and in the past tense *lied*, as in 'Tom is a truthful boy; he has never *lied* to me'.

learn and **teach** The confusion of these two words is fairly common. The use of *learn* in 'I go to school and Miss Jones *learns* me lessons' is wrong. The correct version should be 'I go to school and Miss Jones *teaches* me lessons'. *Learn* means 'to study', while *teach* means 'to instruct'.

like and **as** The use of the word *like* as a conjunction is good English, as you can see in the following examples: 'Anna is very *like* her mother', 'Bill plays the violin *like* a professional', 'This coin looks *like* silver to me'.

It is not good practice to use *like* as a preposition, such as in the sentence 'This room looks *like* it's been hit by a hurricane'. The correct phrase would read, 'This room looks *as if* it's been hit by a hurricane'.

ANNA IS VERY LIKE HER MOTHER

livid and **angry** 'When I got to school yesterday, my teacher was *livid* because I was so late'. The word *livid* is often used to mean 'angry', but it originally meant 'of a greyish tinge or colour'.

mad This word means 'insane, or mentally deranged', but is often used to mean 'angry', particularly in the United States. The second use is an informal one, and is best avoided in written English.

majority This means 'the greater number'. It cannot be used to describe quantities or areas. It is therefore wrong to say: 'The *majority* of Europe was covered by snow'. Instead of *the majority*, you should say *most of*, or *the greater part*. However it is correct

English to say: 'The *majority* of children are more healthy today' because children can be counted as separate things.

malapropism A *malapropism* is a word that sounds similar to another and is used wrongly in its place. It was named after Mrs Malaprop, a character in *The Rivals* by Sheridan. An example of a *malapropism* would be to use 'fertile' instead of 'futile' in the sentence: 'All our efforts are *fertile*'.

mantel and **mantle** The first word means 'the surround to a fireplace', while *mantle* means 'a loose wrap or cloak'.

masterful and **masterly** The first word means 'domineering', and the second means 'skilful'.

may and **might** The word *might* is the past tense of *may*. It expresses possibility in sentences like 'It *may* be fine tomorrow', 'You *might* have been hurt'. In both sentences, *may* could be exchanged for *might* and *might* for *may*, but the meanings of both sentences would be a little different. If I say '*Might* I take you out to dinner?', it sounds a little less certain than '*May* I take you out to dinner?', although both sentences are correct English.

maybe and **may be** The first word is an adverb and means 'perhaps or possibly', as in the sentence '*Maybe* I will be going to the theatre tonight'. *May be*, however, is two verbs, as in the sentence: 'My sister Clare *may be* coming to visit us tomorrow'.

media This word has come into use to describe methods of communication such as newspapers, television and radio and is, in fact, the plural of *medium*. It is therefore wrong to speak of *media* as if it were singular, as in: 'The *media* is responsible for much of the lack of discipline today'. The sentence should read 'The *media* are ...'

mediocre This does not mean 'bad'. It means 'average or ordinary in quality; neither good nor bad'.

meter and **metre** The word *meter* is a device or machine for measuring something. A *metre* is a measurement of length. American custom uses the same spelling, *meter*, for both.

more and **most** It is wrong to say, for instance, 'Jack is the *most* intelligent of my two sons', because when comparing two things you should use the comparative *more*. You cannot have the *most* intelligent of two. However, you should use *most* when speaking of three or more, as in 'There are a lot of bookshops in London and *most* of them are in the West End'.

myself The word *myself* should not be used instead of 'I' or 'me'. The two following sentences are wrong: 'It was kind of you to ask my son and *myself* to your party', 'The members of the society and *myself* waited for a reply'. In the first sentence, *myself* should be replaced by *me*, and in the second, it should be replaced by *I*.

naught and **nought** The word *naught* means 'nothing', but the word *nought* refers to the zero symbol 0. The word *naughty* is taken from *naught*, and originally meant 'good for nothing'.

never means 'not ever' and it is wrong to use it if you are referring to only one occasion, as in 'I *never* met you on the train today'. This sentence should read: 'I did not meet you on the train today'. In the sentence, 'I have *never* been to the British Museum', the word *never* is used correctly.

No. or **no.** This is the standard abbreviation used in English and other European languages for the word *number*. In the United States, the symbol # is commonly used.

no one and **no-one** Either of these two forms can be used, but the two words should never be run together as *noone*.

not only ... but also If you use the expression *not only* it must be balanced by *but also* later in the sentence. For example: 'Jane lost *not only* her scarf, *but also* her gloves', 'We would like *not only* to meet you, *but also* your friend'.

noun A *noun* is the grammatical term for words which are the names of things, animals, ideas and qualities. There are four kinds of *nouns: proper nouns, abstract nouns, collective nouns* and *common nouns (see box for examples).*

A *proper noun* is a special name for a place, thing or person. All proper nouns take capital letters. The days of the week and months of the year are also *proper nouns.*

An *abstract noun* is something which cannot be actually touched, seen or physically felt.

Collective nouns are those which deal with collections of things or persons.

Common nouns include all the rest, a few examples being given here: *house, man, pencil, tree, plate, sky, wood, chalk, coffee, anvil.*

Nouns can sometimes be used as verbs. Here are some examples: 'Joe is going to *paper* his room', 'The engineer came to *service* our dish-washer', 'That is a nasty cut; let me *bandage* it'.

Nouns can also be used as adjectives, as in '*barber* shop', '*birthday* present', '*customer* service', '*soap*-dish'.

Nouns
proper nouns:
Australia
Memphis
New York
William Shakespeare
Shredded Wheat
The White House
Saturday
December

abstract nouns

kindness	truth
terror	pleasure
bravery	honesty
fear	fame
hope	happiness
love	

collective nouns:
a swarm of bees
a herd of cattle
a gaggle of geese
a ship's crew
a fleet of ships
a company of actors
a school of dolphins
a football team
a band of robbers
a clump of trees
a pack of cards
a set of pencils
a litter of kittens
a cluster of trees
a troop of monkeys

occur and **take place** The word *occur* means 'to happen by chance', while *take place* is used when an event or occasion is prearranged. 'An accident *occurred* in the market square' illustrates the first, while 'The wedding will *take place* on Thursday' illustrates the use of the second phrase.

off of This expression is sometimes heard, as in 'I jumped *off of* the platform'. It is incorrect and the word *of* should be omitted.

official and **officious** *Official* means 'formal or authorized', while *officious* means 'interfering or meddlesome'.

only It is important to place the word *only* correctly in a sentence, otherwise the meaning can be quite different. Here are some examples: 'Peter spoke *only* to Caroline' means that Peter spoke to Caroline and nobody else. '*Only* Peter spoke to Caroline' means that it was Peter and no-one else who spoke to Caroline. 'Peter *only* spoke to Caroline' means that Peter did nothing more than speak to Caroline.

-or and **-our** The ending *-our* is usual in such words as *honour, colour, labour, behaviour*. However, there are a number of exceptions. The following words are spelled *-or*: *error, horror, languor, liquor, pallor, squalor, stupor, terror, torpor, tremor*. In the United States, most *-our* ending words are spelled *-or*, but there are exceptions. The word *glamour* is spelled *-our* both in Britain and America.

oral and **aural** These two words are pronounced in almost exactly the same way, but they mean different things. *Oral* means 'spoken, verbal' or 'of the mouth', while *aural* means 'of the ear'. If you attend an *oral examination*, the questions and answers will be spoken out loud. An *aural test* will check your hearing.

outside of The word *outside* should not be followed by *of*. The word *of* should be omitted.

pail and **pale** The first word is a noun and means 'a bucket', and the second word is an adjective and means 'lacking brightness or colour'.

palate, **palette** and **pallet**. *Palate* means 'the roof of the mouth', a *palette* is 'an artist's board for mixing colours', and a *pallet* is 'a portable wooden platform' or 'an instrument used by potters'.

palindrome A *palindrome* is a word, phrase or number, which, if taken in reverse order, will read the same. Here are some palindromes: *Noon; nun; madam; mum; Bob; Madam, I'm Adam; Able was I ere I saw Elba; 1991.*

participle *Participles* are parts of a verb, which are used, together with auxiliary verbs, to form tenses. A *participle* can also be used as an adjective. There are two kinds: *present participles* and *past participles. Present participles* end in *-ing*, as in *jumping, printing, turning, walking. Past participles* usually end in *-d* or *-ed*, as in *heard, jumped, printed, turned, walked.* Sometimes they end in *-n* or *-t*, as in *broken* and *burnt.*

You can use a *present participle* with the auxiliary verb 'to be', as in *I am jumping, he is printing, she was turning, they were walking.* You can use a *past participle* with the auxiliary verb 'to have', as in *I have jumped, he has printed, she has turned, they have walked.*

Participles can also be used as adjectives, as in 'the *burnt* paper', 'the *broken* cup', 'the *jumping* horse', 'the *printed* book', 'the *turning* wheel', 'the *walking* doll'.

passed and **past** *Passed* is a verb (the past tense of *pass*), and is used in such sentences as 'You have *passed* my house', 'Father has *passed* the age of sixty', 'Many years have now *passed*'. The word *past* can be a noun, an adjective or a preposition: 'History tells what happened in the *past*' [noun]; 'There has been very bad weather during the *past* week' [adjective]; 'The bus drove straight *past*' [preposition].

pedal and **peddle** A *pedal* is a lever operated by the foot, and *peddle* is a verb, and means 'to go from place to place selling things'.

peninsula and **peninsular**. The first word is a noun and means 'a piece of land almost surrounded by water'. The second word is an adjective and means 'of, or like, a peninsula'.

pidgin and **pigeon** The first word describes a kind of trading language used in the South Seas, and the second word describes a kind of bird.

perestroika This is a Russian word which has only recently come into the English language. It means 'reconstruction or reform'.

plain and **plane** The first word, *plain*, means 'clear, distinct or straight-forward', while *plane* can mean either 'a flat surface'or 'a kind of tree'. It is also used as an abbreviated version of 'aeroplane'.

plurals The *plural* in English (that is, when more than one person or thing is named) is usually formed by adding an *s* to the noun, as in: book, *books*; hand, *hands*; house, *houses*; tree, *trees*; way, *ways*. Words ending in *ch, s, sh, x,* and *z* add *es* for the *plural*, as in church, *churches*; loss, *losses*; bush, *bushes*; box, *boxes*; fizz, *fizzes*.

When a noun ends in *y* with a consonant before it, the *y* is changed to an *i*, as in baby, *babies*; lady, *ladies*; story, *stories*; company, *companies*; history, *histories*. If a vowel comes before the *y*, the *plural* usually remains as *s*, as in boy, *boys*; storey, *storeys*; tray, *trays*.

Most nouns ending with *f* or *fe* change the *f* or *fe* into *v* and add *es*, as in leaf, *leaves*; wolf, *wolves*; thief, *thieves*; wife, *wives*. There are exceptions; the following words keep the *f* and add an *s*: belief, *beliefs*; chief, *chiefs*; dwarf, *dwarfs*; reef, *reefs*; roof, *roofs*.

Common words ending in *o* take *es* as a *plural*, as in cargo, *cargoes*; potato, *potatoes*; hero, *heroes*; tomato, *tomatoes*; echo, *echoes*. There are many others, however, which simply add *s*: commando, *commandos*; dynamo, *dynamos*; piano, *pianos*; radio, *radios*.

There are some *irregular plurals*. Certain words, such as *deer, cod, sheep, salmon, aircraft, measles, scissors* remain the same, whether singular or *plural*. Some words form their *plural* by adding *en*, as in ox, *oxen*; child, *children*; man, *men*; woman, *women*. Yet other words become *plural* by changing the vowel or vowels in the middle of the word, as in foot, *feet*; tooth, *teeth*; goose, *geese*; mouse, *mice*.

possessive adjectives The *possessive* of an adjective shows who something or someone belongs to. It is formed by the use of the words *his, hers, its, my, our, their, your,* as used in such sentences as '*My* car has *its* difficulties', 'Where is *our* car?', 'I have met *your* friend', 'You must keep *your* temper'. The word *whose* is both a *possessive adjective* and a possessive pronoun, as in: 'The girl *whose* bicycle I borrowed is my friend' [possessive adjective]; and 'I borrowed a bicycle, but I didn't know *whose*' [possessive pronoun].

possessive nouns The *possessive* form of a noun is usually shown by adding *'s* or *s'*. In the case of a single noun, add *'s*, as in *the boy's book, the girl's dress, Peter's house*. If the noun is singular, but ends in *s*, add *'s*, as in *the princess's tour, the rhinoceros's horn, the platypus's bill, St James's Square*.

Words ending in *x* or *z* are treated in the same way: *Max's restaurant, Liz's scarf*. If the noun is plural and ends in *s*, add an apostrophe only: *the teachers' room, the soldiers' uniforms*. If the noun is plural, but does not end in *s*, add *'s*, as in *the children's toys, the men's room, the women's club*. Words ending in *es* are treated as if they were plural nouns and only an apostrophe is added: *Moses' people*.

THE RHINOCEROS'S HORN

possessive pronouns The *possessive* of pronouns is formed by the use of the words: *hers, its, mine, ours, theirs, whose, yours*, as in 'That car is *theirs*', 'This pen is *mine*', 'Which dress is *hers*?'. An apostrophe is not used in these cases, so it is wrong to write: *her's, it's, our's, their's, who's, your's* [*it's* and *who's* mean *it is* and *who is*].

practicable and **practical** The first word means 'possible, feasible, able to be put into practice', and the second means 'workable, useful, adapted to actual conditions'.

pray and **prey** The word *pray* means 'to offer a prayer', and *prey* means 'an animal hunted for food'.

precede and **proceed** *Precede* means 'to go or come before', and *proceed* means 'to carry on, to progress'.

precedent and **president** The first word means 'an example or instance used in law', while the second means 'the head of a state, republic or company'.

prefix This is placed before a word to form a new word. The following are commonly used *prefixes*: *ex-* means 'out of' or 'former', as in *export*, or *ex-president*; *pre-* means 'before in time or position', as in *prehistoric*; *re-* means 'to return or do again' as in *return* or *rewind*; *un-* and *dis-* denote reversal of an action, as in *undress* and *disapprove*; *non-* denotes a negative, as in *non-member*.

preposition A *preposition* is a word used with a noun (or the equivalent of a noun) to show the position or relation of the noun to other words (*see box for examples*). Sometimes, several words together can form a *preposition*, such as *with regard to; up to; in respect of; onto;*

in accordance with. *Prepositions* link and introduce phrases, and show direction or relationship. 'Mr Brown realized that his wife was *out* of the house, and drove the car *into* town', 'I shall remain here *until* February'.

There is an old rule which says that a sentence should never end with a *preposition*. In fact, *prepositions* should go before the noun, but sometimes it is not possible to write a sentence without ending it with a *preposition*. Sir Winston Churchill made a joke of the rule by writing 'this is the sort of English *up with* which I will not put'.

Sentences ending with a *preposition* can be used when necessary but there are some which sound wrong. Here is one which ends with no fewer than three prepositions: 'What did you choose that book to be read *out of for*?'. If a sentence sounds wrong, it almost certainly *is* wrong.

principal and **principle** The word *principal* means 'chief, leading, main'

prepositions	
after	of
at	on
before	out
by	over
down	through
for	to
from	until
in	up
into	with

and the second word, *principle*, means 'a general truth, law or standard'.

prise and **prize** The first word is a verb and means 'to force open', while the second, as a noun, means 'a reward'. *Prize* can be a verb meaning 'to value greatly', and it can also be another spelling of the first word *prise*.

prone means 'lying face downward'.

pronoun A *pronoun* is a word used instead of, or to replace a noun. The following words are all *pronouns*: *I, me,*

PREY
PRAYING

she, him, her, one, it, you, we, us, they, them. These are called *personal pronouns*. There are four other kinds: relative *pronouns* – *who, whose, whom, which, that*; possessive *pronouns* – *mine, yours, his, hers, its, ours, theirs*; interrogative *pronouns* – *what, who, which, whom, whose*; and demonstrative *pronouns* – *this, these, that, those, the other, others, such, the same*. (*See box*.)

---

pronouns

personal pronoun:
'Mr Smith owns a shop. *He* sells sweets.'

relative pronoun:
'Mr Smith is the owner of the shop *that* sells sweets.'

possessive pronoun:
'This sweet shop is *his*.'

interrogative pronoun:
'*What* does this shop sell?'

demonstrative pronoun:
'*This* belongs to Mr Smith.'

---

question mark [?] This is a mark of punctuation, and is used instead of a full stop at the end of direct 'question' sentences. *What is your name? How shall I get to your house? When will the next lesson be?* In dialogue, that is, when you are writing down someone's conversation, you should enclose the statement in quotation marks and include the *question mark* inside the quotation: '"*Would you like an ice-*

cream?" asked Mary', '"*What time does the train leave?*" enquired Sam'. In these cases, the following word (*asked* and *enquired*) does not need a capital letter.

quiet and **quite** Although they are pronounced differently, these two words are sometimes confused. *Quiet* means 'calm and tranquil', and *quite* means 'completely and absolutely'.

quire and **choir** Both these words have a similar pronunciation, but are spelled differently. *Quire* is a measurement for a quantity of paper, and a *choir* is a group of singers.

quotation marks [' '] or [" "] These are used at the beginning and at the end of something that is quoted, such as conversation. *Quotation marks* are either single [' '] or double [" "] inverted commas. ''Don't be silly,' said Alice', '"What a lovely day!" exclaimed the March Hare'. The *quotation marks* are placed only at the beginning and end of the actual sentence or phrase quoted.

"DON'T BE SILLY"
SAID ALICE

SKULL SCULLING

raise and **raze** The first word is a verb meaning 'to move to a higher position', and the second word is also a verb, but means 'to demolish completely'.

rapt, **rapped** and **wrapped** *Rapt* is an adjective, and means 'totally absorbed or engrossed', *rapped* is a verb, the past tense of 'to rap', while *wrapped* is the past tense of the verb 'to wrap', and means 'to enfold or cover'.

recount and **re-count** The first word means 'to tell a story', and the second means 'to count again'.

redolent means 'odorous' or 'smelling of'.

reflexive pronouns The following are *reflexive pronouns: myself, yourself, himself, herself, oneself, itself, ourselves, yourselves, themselves.* They are used to refer to the subject of the clause or sentence in which they are found. Here are some examples: 'I ate the apples *myself*', 'he found *himself* back on the road', 'you can do that job *yourself*', 'we all enjoyed *ourselves*'.

reform and **re-form** The first word means 'to improve or correct', and the second word means 'to form anew'.

reign and **rein** To *reign* means 'to rule or exercise power', while a *rein* is 'one of a pair of straps used to control a horse'.

review and **revue** A *review* is a report or essay, but a *revue* is a theatrical performance.

rhyme and **rime** *Rhyme* means a word-ending which sounds like another, and *rime* means 'frost'. This last spelling was used once for both words.

said When you are writing dialogue, that is, words spoken by a character in a story, the style is usually like this: '"Please come in and sit down," *said* Mr Evans'. The word *said* can be used as many times as required but it can also be replaced by many other 'verbs of speaking', for example: *whispered, spluttered, smiled, grinned, shouted, called, asked, demanded, queried, replied, exclaimed, ordered, screamed, grumbled, complained, reminded.*

sceptic and **septic** The word *sceptic* means 'someone who distrusts or disbelieves people', while *septic* means 'infected by bacteria'. The first word is pronounced 'skeptic', which is the way the word is spelled in the United States.

scull and **skull** To *scull* means 'to row a boat', while *skull* means 'the bones of the head'.

29

semi-colon [;] This is a punctuation mark. It is used when something stronger than a comma, but less strong than a full stop, is needed. Usually it is used to link two parts of a sentence which are not already linked by a conjunction, as in: 'The car wouldn't start; its battery was flat', 'The snow fell heavily; it covered roof-tops everywhere', 'The girl ran quickly; she wanted to escape'.

sew and **sow** The word *sew* means 'to use needle and thread', while *sow* means 'to scatter seed'.

simile *Similes* are figures of speech, in which one thing is compared with another, such as in *dead as a doornail; deaf as a post; mad as a hatter; red as a beetroot*. These are *similes*, but they are also clichés and best avoided. These are some more acceptable examples of *similes*: 'Her *cheek* was *like damask*; her *hair as* spun *gold*', 'As soon as Ben saw his angry father, he shot out of his *chair like a rocket*'.

stationary and **stationery** The first word means 'not moving, standing still', and the second word means 'writing materials'.

stile and **style** A *stile* is a set of steps over and through a fence, and *style* means 'form or appearance'.

storey and **story** The word *storey* means 'a floor or level of a building', and *story* means 'a tale or yarn'. The plural of *storey* is *storeys*; that of *story* is *stories*. In the United States, both words are usually spelled 'story'.

straight and **strait** The word *straight* means 'not curved or crooked', and the word *strait* means 'a narrow channel of the sea'.

suffix A *suffix* is placed at the end of a word to form a new one. Here are some *suffixes: -able, -ible, -al, -ance, -dom, -ful, -ish, -less, -ment, -ness*. The following are some examples of words using the *suffixes* mentioned: *liable, sensible, usual, kingdom, thoughtful, boyish, fearless, payment, silliness*. There is a large number of *suffixes*, each one of which has a special purpose to change the meaning of a noun.

swam and **swum** The word *swam* is the past tense of the verb to *swim*, and is used as in the sentence: 'Dick *swam* across the river'. The word *swum* should not be used in such a way, since it is a *past participle* and needs the auxiliary verb 'to have'. Here is an example of its use: 'Several people *had swum* across the lake'.

synonyms	
abbreviate	shorten
abundant	plentiful
apparition	ghost
attire	dress
begin	commence
bravery	courage
brief	short
choice	option
conclusion	ending
courteous	polite
difficult	hard
enemy	foe
hatred	loathing
huge	enormous
inside	interior
rarely	seldom
sly	cunning
suspend	hang
thankful	grateful
unite	join

synonym A *synonym* is a word which has a similar, or closely related meaning to another word (*see box*). English words do not have exact *synonyms*, although some are very close in meaning to others. The word *fast*, for instance, means almost the same as *quick* but the two words cannot always be interchanged. You would speak of a '*fast* car', but not of a '*quick* car'.

tautology means unnecessary repetition of an idea. Here are some examples: 'Sally has drawn a *four-sided square* on her paper'. All squares are four-sided, so the words 'four-sided' should be omitted. 'Everyone knows that Columbus discovered America. It's *past history!*' History is in the past anyway, so the word 'past' is not needed. 'A *free gift* with every new bike!' A gift is something given free of charge therefore you do not need the word 'free'. Here are a few expressions commonly used, but which are *tautological: added bonus; all alone; check up; close down; divide up; end result; finish up; later on; over again; refer back; settle up; true facts; unite together.*

their, **there** and **they're** The first word means 'belonging to them', and the second means 'in that place', while the third is a contraction of the two words *they are*.

times and dates It is very important, when writing down a *time* or a *date*, that the reader should be in no doubt as to its meaning. *Times* should be clear: *9 a.m.* (not *9.00 a.m.*), *10.30 p.m., half-past six, five o'clock*. If the 24-hour clock is used, then *times* should be shown as: *9.00 hrs., 11.30 hrs., 18.20 hrs., 23.10 hrs.* Dates should be clear, too. The simplest method is *date, month, year,* as in *14 October 1978*. It is best to avoid writing *dates* in the form *12/10/89* or *12.10.89*. In Great Britain, this would be read as: *12 October, 1989,* but in the United States it would be read as: *December 10, 1989.*

tire and **tyre** The word *tire* means 'to become fatigued or weary', and *tyre* means 'the rim of a wheel'. In the United States the first spelling is used for both words.

troop and **troupe** The word *troop* is used to describe a unit in an army, while *troupe* is applied to a group of actors or performers.

unique means 'the only one of its kind, without equal or like', so you cannot say *almost unique, fairly unique* or *quite unique.*

unwanted and **unwonted** The first word means 'not wanted', and the second means 'unusual or out of the ordinary'.

verb A *verb* is a part of speech which asks a question, expresses a command, and tells what someone or something does or is. *Verbs* can tell you about the past, in the past tense, the present, in

31

the present tense, and the future, in the future tense. Here is a *verb*, showing the parts of speech and the three tenses:

Present	Past	Future
I jump	I jumped	I will jump
You jump	You jumped	You will jump
He jumps	He jumped	He will jump
She jumps	She jumped	She will jump
We jump	We jumped	We will jump
They jump	They jumped	They will jump

Verbs are divided into transitive and intransitive *verbs*. A transitive *verb* always needs an object; it does something *to* something. For example the *verb 'to hit'* is a transitive *verb*; you must hit something, 'I *hit* the floor'. Intransitive *verbs* do not require an object. The *verb 'to sleep'* is intransitive, since you cannot *sleep* anything; you just sleep.

Auxiliary *verbs* are 'helping' *verbs*; they are used with other *verbs*. The usual auxiliary *verbs* are *to be*, *to have* and *to do*. Here are some examples of auxiliary *verbs*: '*I am* walking to Oxford in aid of Oxfam', 'Those boxes *are* not wanted on the voyage', '*She has* asked me to call round this evening', '*I do* not wish to be disturbed'.

W

waive and **wave** *Waive* means 'to set aside, or to give up something', and *wave* means 'to flutter, or signal with something'.

wander and **wonder** The word *wander* means 'to move about in an irregular way', while *wonder* means 'something strange or exciting', but it is also a verb which means 'to ponder or think about'.

Y

yoke and **yolk** The word *yoke* means 'a wooden neck-piece for oxen', and *yolk* means 'the yellow part of an egg'.